Companion. Peace.

The Workbook to Accompany
*Same Sh*t. Different Date.*

Why You Keep Attracting The Same Wrong Partners –

And How To Finally Solve It!

*This book is dedicated to my
beloved wife, Katrina.*

Same Sh*t. Different Date.

Copyright ©2019 by Dave Elliott Legendary Love Publishing Company,
a division of MPower Unlimited, Incorporated

All rights reserved. No reproduction of this book, in whole or in part, or in any form may be made without exclusive permission from the copyright owner.

Published in the USA

The following are trademarks belonging exclusively to Dave Elliott and Legendary Love Publishing Company, a division of MPower Unlimited, Incorporated:

R.O.O.T.

C.O.R.E.

H.E.A.R.T.

H.E.A.R.T. Flips

Legendary Love for Life

12 Traumatic M.I.S.B.E.H.A.V.I.O.R.S.

The 8 F's of Personal Transformation

Companion. Peace.
The Workbook to Accompany
*Same Sh*t. Different Date.*

**Why You Keep Attracting The Same Wrong Partners –
And How To Finally Solve It!**

Chapter 1: The Hidden Gifts in Your Relationships

Chapter 2: Getting Down to the R.O.O.T. of the C.O.R.E.

Chapter 3: Here We Go Again…or Why the Hell Does This Keep Happening?!?

Chapter 4: SoulMate or Soul Messenger?

Chapter 5: Magical Morphing Messengers

Chapter 6: "My Ex Did A Number On Me" - How To Identify Recurring Patterns

Chapter 7: Uncover Your Soul Messenger Matrix: Freedom Awaits in Your H.E.A.R.T.™

Chapter 8: Into the Matrix - Revealed: New Awareness for Old Issues

Chapter 9: The ABC's of Healing

Chapter 10: Same Old Story, Brand New Happy Ending

Chapter 11: Knowing and Showing Your Value: The 8 F's of Personal Transformation

Chapter 12: Growing Your Greatness: The 8 F's of Personal Transformation

Chapter 13: The Past May Predict Your Future but It's not Predetermined

Appendix

About the Author

Chapter 1:

The Hidden Gifts In Your Relationships

Your Chapter Notes:

_____
_____
_____
_____
_____
_____
_____
_____
_____

Instead of asking "why did they do that?" ask
⇨ **"what was my role in that?"**

Instead of asking "why do they make me feel this way?" ask
⇨ **"what is this triggering in me?"**

Instead of asking "why does this always happen to me" ask
⇨ **"what can I learn from this?"**

Chapter 2:

Getting Down To The R.O.O.T.™ Of The C.O.R.E.™

R.O.O.T. Issues Lead To C.O.R.E. Wounds™

R.O.O.T. stands for Relationship Origin Of Trauma

C.O.R.E. Wounds are based on Continuous Or Recurring Experiences.

Your Chapter Notes:

_____
_____
_____
_____
_____
_____
_____
_____
_____

Use this quick checklist to identify some of the common signs and symptoms of ROOT issues:

R.O.O.T. issues for singles:
- Do you struggle in relationships?
- Do you feel jaded about the topic of love itself?
- Do you attract the same wrong partners again and again?
- Does it seem like no matter what, you just can't find love?
- Do you struggle to even find a date?!?
- Is relationship too painful to even think about?
- Have you already given up on love?
- Are you afraid you don't even deserve love?
- Do you put up walls with prospective partners?
- Do uncontrollable emotions sabotage you?
- Are you afraid people will leave you?

R.O.O.T. issues for couples:
- Do you feel tender or sometimes walk on eggshells with your partner?
- Do you get more and more guarded or put up walls with others?
- Do you find yourself getting or staying angry at one another?
- Have you lost confidence or radiance, or have you never had it in your relationship?
- Do you feel like you lost your faith in people, or in your love?
- Are you starting to think you'll never have love even though you are in a relationship?
- Or worse yet…are you afraid you don't even deserve love?

If you answered yes to any of those things…I PROMISE you that a ROOT issue is sabotaging you right now in real time. And I also promise you…this book holds the answer you seek. Read on…

Chapter 3:

Here We Go Again… or why the hell does this keep happening?!?

Your Chapter Notes:

_____

_____

_____

_____

_____

_____

_____

_____

_____

Chapter 4:

Soul Mate or Soul Messenger? They Both Come To Serve

Your Chapter Notes:

_____
_____
_____
_____
_____
_____
_____
_____
_____
_____

Chapter 5:

Magical Morphing Messengers

Your Chapter Notes:

_____
_____
_____
_____
_____
_____
_____
_____
_____
_____

Chapter 6:

"My Ex Did A Number On Me" – How to Identify Recurring Patterns

Your Chapter Notes:

_____
_____
_____
_____
_____
_____
_____
_____
_____
_____

Let's Identify Any Recurring Patterns From Your Past Partnerships

Partner name: _____ Scenario: ____
Significant memories/clues: _____
Relevant Number List: _____
_____

1 2 3 4 5 6 7 8 9 10 11 12 13 14 15 16 17 18 19 20 21 22
23 24 25 26 27 28 29 30 31 32 33 34 35 36 37 38 39 40
41 42 43 44 45 46 47 48 49 50 51 52 53 54

Partner name: _____ Scenario: ____
Significant memories/clues: _____
Relevant Number List: _____
_____

1 2 3 4 5 6 7 8 9 10 11 12 13 14 15 16 17 18 19 20 21 22
23 24 25 26 27 28 29 30 31 32 33 34 35 36 37 38 39 40
41 42 43 44 45 46 47 48 49 50 51 52 53 54

Partner name: _____ Scenario: ____
Significant memories/clues: _____
Relevant Number List: _____
_____

1 2 3 4 5 6 7 8 9 10 11 12 13 14 15 16 17 18 19 20 21 22
23 24 25 26 27 28 29 30 31 32 33 34 35 36 37 38 39 40
41 42 43 44 45 46 47 48 49 50 51 52 53 54

Partner name: _____ Scenario: ____
Significant memories/clues: _____
Relevant Number List: _____
_____

1 2 3 4 5 6 7 8 9 10 11 12 13 14 15 16 17 18 19 20 21 22
23 24 25 26 27 28 29 30 31 32 33 34 35 36 37 38 39 40
41 42 43 44 45 46 47 48 49 50 51 52 53 54

Partner name: _____ Scenario: ____
Significant memories/clues: _____
Relevant Number List: _____
_____

1 2 3 4 5 6 7 8 9 10 11 12 13 14 15 16 17 18 19 20 21 22
23 24 25 26 27 28 29 30 31 32 33 34 35 36 37 38 39 40
41 42 43 44 45 46 47 48 49 50 51 52 53 54

Partner name: _____ Scenario: ____
Significant memories/clues: _____
Relevant Number List: _____
_____

1 2 3 4 5 6 7 8 9 10 11 12 13 14 15 16 17 18 19 20 21 22
23 24 25 26 27 28 29 30 31 32 33 34 35 36 37 38 39 40
41 42 43 44 45 46 47 48 49 50 51 52 53 54

Partner name: _____ Scenario: ____
Significant memories/clues: _____
Relevant Number List: _____
_____

1 2 3 4 5 6 7 8 9 10 11 12 13 14 15 16 17 18 19 20 21 22
23 24 25 26 27 28 29 30 31 32 33 34 35 36 37 38 39 40
41 42 43 44 45 46 47 48 49 50 51 52 53 54

Partner name: _____ Scenario: ____
Significant memories/clues: _____
Relevant Number List: _____
_____

1 2 3 4 5 6 7 8 9 10 11 12 13 14 15 16 17 18 19 20 21 22
23 24 25 26 27 28 29 30 31 32 33 34 35 36 37 38 39 40
41 42 43 44 45 46 47 48 49 50 51 52 53 54

Partner name: _____ Scenario: ____
Significant memories/clues: _____
Relevant Number List: _____
_____

1 2 3 4 5 6 7 8 9 10 11 12 13 14 15 16 17 18 19 20 21 22
23 24 25 26 27 28 29 30 31 32 33 34 35 36 37 38 39 40
41 42 43 44 45 46 47 48 49 50 51 52 53 54

Partner name: _____ Scenario: ____
Significant memories/clues: _____
Relevant Number List: _____
_____

1 2 3 4 5 6 7 8 9 10 11 12 13 14 15 16 17 18 19 20 21 22
23 24 25 26 27 28 29 30 31 32 33 34 35 36 37 38 39 40
41 42 43 44 45 46 47 48 49 50 51 52 53 54

Partner name: _____ Scenario: ____
Significant memories/clues: _____
Relevant Number List: _____
_____

1 2 3 4 5 6 7 8 9 10 11 12 13 14 15 16 17 18 19 20 21 22
23 24 25 26 27 28 29 30 31 32 33 34 35 36 37 38 39 40
41 42 43 44 45 46 47 48 49 50 51 52 53 54

Partner name: _____ Scenario: ____
Significant memories/clues: _____
Relevant Number List: _____
_____

1 2 3 4 5 6 7 8 9 10 11 12 13 14 15 16 17 18 19 20 21 22
23 24 25 26 27 28 29 30 31 32 33 34 35 36 37 38 39 40
41 42 43 44 45 46 47 48 49 50 51 52 53 54

Identifying Recurring Patterns

Circle THE NUMBER of any experience below that applies to you:

(1) Divorce
(2) Separation
(3) Death
(4) Incarceration
(5) Drug rehab
(6) Infidelity
(7) Family/Custody disputes
(8) Adoption
(9) Isolation
(10) Rejection
(11) Long distance romance
(12) Military service
(13) Job transfer
(14) Ghosted
(15) Sustained infrequent contact
(16) Non-payment of support
(17) Domestic violence
(18) Cyberbullying
(19) Humiliation
(20) Objectification
(21) Name calling
(22) Criticism/attacks
(23) Verbal threats
(24) Intimidation
(25) Manipulation
(26) Injustice
(27) Shame
(28) Betrayal
(29) Exploitation
(30) Massive uncertainty
(31) Distant/disinterested
(32) Gossiping
(33) Spreading lies or innuendo
(34) Substance abuse
(35) Sexual assault
(36) Mental illness
(37) Assault & battery
(38) Addictions
(39) Neglect
(40) Emotional abuse
(41) Narcissism
(42) Personality disorders
(43) Rage/anger issues
(44) Communication issues
(45) Promiscuity cheating
(46) Eviction
(47) Adoption
(48) Foster care
(49) Step-parents
(50) Accidents
(51) Fire
(52) Floods
(53) Natural disasters
(54) War/terror

Connecting The Dots

Like any good 'connect-the-dots' exercise, we will use the numbers provided next to each possible answer and connect them in order to reveal the bigger picture represented by the numbers and their placement. However, you won't actually be drawing lines on a page to reveal that hidden picture. In this exercise, the numbers you connect, themselves, will give you a very clear picture of everything you need to see when you follow my directions properly. I've set it up this way to simplify it for you when it comes to immediately seeing patterns so be sure to circle the number next to any word you did experience. For instance, the first answer in the list below just happens to be the word "divorce." So the question you will ask yourself is:

- **As a child, did I experience a <u>divorce?</u>**

Obviously, I'm not talking about your divorce if you were only a child. I'm asking if your parents or primary caretakers experienced a divorce that affected YOU. If it did, you would circle the corresponding number 1 that goes with that answer. If it does not apply to you, simply skip that and move through the rest of list circling or writing down the numbers you experienced.

Write any numbers that apply here: _____

_____

_____

Step Two

Next we're going to skip ahead and start to scan our prior relationships giving particular emphasis to marriages, engagements, or live-in partners. We want to prioritize for those significant partners who were closest to you or lived with you or in close proximity. Then, let's identify any past partners based on duration of time together or emotional closeness. Let's also be sure to identify by name and include any partners who represented a significant emotional investment or even a painful breakup. The rule of thumb here is that the stronger the emotion you attach to the person, the stronger the clue. So do some digging. This is where we start to mine for the clues that will help you change everything.

Here's an example of what your evaluation will look like when finished:

Partner name: __Don__ Scenario: __2__
Significant memories/clues: __Ex-husband, infidelity__
Relevant Number List: __1, 2, 3, 6, 10, 12, 16, 21, 25,
28, 30, 31, 44, 45__
①②③4 5⑥7 8 9 ⑩ 11 ⑫ 13 14 15 ⑯ 17 18 19 20 ㉑ 22
23 24 25 26 27 ㉘ 29 ㉚㉛ 32 33 34 35 36 37 38 39 40
41 42 43 ㊹㊺ 46 47 48 49 50 51 52 53 54

Partner name: __Jason__ Scenario: __3__
Significant memories/clues: __Former fiance, wedding called off__
Relevant Number List: __2, 4, 6, 10, 11, 12, 17, 21, 22, 25,
28, 30, 31, 34, 44, 45__
1②3④5⑥7 8 9 ⑩⑪⑫ 13 14 15 16 ⑰ 18 19 20 ㉑㉒
23 24 ㉕ 26 27 ㉘ 29 ㉚㉛ 32 33 ㉞ 35 36 37 38 39 40
41 42 43 ㊹㊺ 46 47 48 49 50 51 52 53 54

What was your number total?

Once you have completed the assignment for each former partner you've identified, first, let's note how many scenarios we reviewed to get that number. Remember, that would include both your own childhood which was scenario # 1 and then an additional scenario for each former significant other you evaluated. So if you assessed your own childhood + 6 individual partners, your baseline number (or the denominator if presented as part of a fraction) would be the number 7. We'll need this number on the assessment so be sure you identify it.

Childhood scenario #__1__ + __6__ former partner scenarios = __7__

Next, let's go back and circle or count all common numbers and track how many times each number gets circled. Remember, if, for example, you circle the number 1 three times, you would note it in the key below as 3/7 - (3 instances out of 7 scenarios).

(1) Divorce _____	(2) Separation _____	(3) Death _____
(4) Incarceration _____	(5) Drug rehab _____	(6) Infidelity _____
(7) Family/Custody disputes _____	(8) Adoption _____	(9) Isolation _____
(10) Rejection _____	(11) Long distance romance _____	(12) military service _____
(13) job transfer _____	(14) Ghosted _____	(15) Sustained infrequent contact _____
(16) non-payment of support _____	(17) Domestic violence _____	(18) cyberbullying _____
(19) Humiliation _____	(20) Objectification _____	(21) Name calling _____
(22) Criticism/attacks _____	(23) Verbal threats _____	(24) Intimidation _____
(25) Manipulation _____	(26) Injustice _____	(27) Shame _____
(28) Betrayal _____	(29) Exploitation _____	(30) Massive uncertainty _____
(31) Distant/disinterested _____	(32) Gossiping _____	(33) Spreading lies/innuendo _____
(34) Substance abuse _____	(35) Sexual assault _____	(36) Mental illness _____
(37) Assault & battery _____	(38) Addictions. _____	(39) Neglect _____
(40) Emotional abuse _____	(41) Narcissism _____	(42) Personality disorders _____
(43) Rage/Anger issues _____	(44) Communication issues _____	(45) Promiscuity/cheating _____
(46) Eviction _____	(47) Adoption _____	(48) Foster care _____
(49) Step-parents _____	(50) Accidents _____	(51) Fire _____
(52) Floods _____	(53) Natural Disasters _____	(54) War/Terror. _____

If you start to notice the same numbers popping up again and again as you rate individual former partners, you have just discovered a recurring issue that is trending across multiple partnerships. Any time a specific number pops up again and again on every single partnership, that qualifies as a pattern that simply cannot be ignored. You'll want to definitely note all of those by finding the highest numbers but, of course, count the smaller numbers as well. Any time a number shows up across the board or in this case, 7 out of 7 scenarios, that is a red flag that you should definitely note and work on later in the book.

Identifying Categories

Once you've gone through and identified the numbers for all your past partners, it's time to look for the over-arching themes that may be recurring again and again. For your convenience and ease of use, this simple diagnostic tool will help you identify at a glance what you need to know. I clustered the issues and numbered them based on some of the most common unresolved wounds. In this case, they all fit into a simple A thru E answer key that breaks down as follows:

Answers of 1 - 16 are related to possible **Abandonment Issues**

Answers of 17 - 24 are related to possible **Bullying Issues**

Answers of 25 - 34 are related to possible **Chaos Issues**

Answers of 35 - 45 are related to possible **Dysfunctional Issues**

Answers of 46 - 54 are related to possible **Environmental Issues**

How many of these recurring issues did you count?

Abandonment Issues _____   Bullying Issues _____

Chaos Issues _____   Dysfunctional Issues _____

Environmental Issues _____

What was your role in that?

Since I've created this checklist of behaviors to grade everyone else, maybe it's a great idea to do a little self-evaluation to determine if there are any areas that you may need or want to improve? Take this quick opportunity to go through my list one more time and see if there are any issues you'd like to improve for your self. Of course, some of these won't apply at all because they were designed to show cross-contextual ways the five different themes show up and cause problems. I intentionally masked them among some other bad habits or sabotaging behaviors that ruin relationships. So let's take one more look before we move on to see if there are some areas where the high performer in you may want to up their game. Maybe you've engaged in (6) Infidelity in the past and you just want to commit to taking that off the table for you in the future based on principle. That would be huge. Or maybe you know you've engaged in (21) Name calling in the past and you just want to commit to not doing that because you know how much you hate it when someone does that to you. That would be a wonderful commitment. Perhaps you see that you may have inadvertently engaged in (14) Ghosting by just fading away over time and you want to be more resolute in your (44) Communication when you don't see a future with someone you've dated. The point is, high-value people get to be high-value by setting high standards for themselves. If that becomes one of your takeaways from this book, I honor you and salute your willingness to own your own role in any past challenges, and commit to changing your own behavior.

Circle **THE NUMBER** of any experience below that applies to you:

(1) Divorce (2) Separation (3) Death
(4) Incarceration (5) Drug rehab (6) Infidelity
(7) Family/Custody disputes (8) Adoption (9) Isolation
(10) Rejection (11) Long distance romance (12) military service
(13) job transfer (14) Ghosted (15) Sustained infrequent contact
(16) non-payment of support (17) Domestic violence (18) cyberbullying
(19) Humiliation (20) Objectification (21) Name calling
(22) Criticism/attacks (23) Verbal threats (24) Intimidation
(25) Manipulation (26) Injustice (27) Shame
(28) Betrayal (29) Exploitation (30) Massive uncertainty
(31) Distant/disinterested (32) Gossiping (33) Spreading lies or innuendo
(34) Substance abuse (35) Sexual assault (36) Mental illness
(37) Assault & battery (38) Addictions (39) Neglect
(40) Emotional abuse (41) Narcissism (42) Personality disorders
(43) Rage/Anger issues (44) Communication issues (45) Promiscuity/cheating
(46) Eviction (47) Adoption (48) Foster care
(49) Step-parents (50) Accidents (51) Fire
(52) Floods (53) Natural Disasters (54) War/Terror

What's your commitment that you're committed to changing in yourself?

Chapter 7:

Uncover Your Soul Messenger Matrix:

Freedom Awaits In Your H.E.A.R.T.™

Your Chapter Notes:

_____
_____
_____
_____
_____
_____
_____
_____
_____

The Soul Messenger Matrix

Simply follow your H.E.A.R.T.™ to where FREEDOM Awaits!

The H stands for HURTS

Name 3 childhood HURTS, disappointments or negative traits of the people who raised you. This might include traits like critical, unavailable, abusive or any number of possibilities.

1) _____

2) _____   **A**

3) _____

(Extra credit answers?) _____

The E stands for EMPATHIC EXPECTATIONS or EMOTIONS

In regard to the 3 childhood HURTS, what did you hope for instead? This would most likely be the opposite of your answers to question number one and include answers like safe, good enough, loved, etc.

1) _____

2) _____   **B**

3) _____

(Extra credit answers?) _____

The A stands for ASSUMPTIONS

As a result of those 3 childhood hurts in question 1, what assumptions did you make about yourself and your own value or inherent worth in light of those hurts? Some possible answers might include that you weren't good or smart enough, you were the wrong body weight, not attractive enough, etc. Any of these possibilities could lead to feelings of shame, guilt, rejection or abandonment.

1) _____

2). _____ C

3). _____

(Extra credit answers?) _____

The R stands for REACTIONS

As a result of those 3 childhood hurts and any other frustrations, how did you respond and what patterns of behavior showed up when you were frustrated? For instance, did you retreat and get quiet, yell, act destructively or self harm? Write down whatever you recall.

1) _____

2). _____ D

3). _____

(Extra credit answers?) _____

The T stands for TRIGGERS

As a result of those 3 childhood hurts, what actions or patterns demonstrated by others provoke those old wounds and create an emotional reaction? Some possible answers might include criticism, being ignored, getting yelled at, disrespected or a range of other possibilities.

1) _____

2). _____ E

3). _____

(Extra credit answers?) _____

Chapter 8:

Into The Matrix - Revealed:
New Awareness For Old Issues

Your Chapter Notes:

_____
_____
_____
_____
_____
_____
_____
_____
_____
_____

Dave Elliott's H.E.A.R.T. Assessment

Simply follow your H.E.A.R.T.™ to where FREEDOM Awaits!

The H stands for HURTS

The E stands for EMPATHIC EXPECTATIONS or EMOTIONS

The A stands for ASSUMPTIONS

The R stands for REACTIONS

The T stands for TRIGGERS

In order to understand the diagnostic tool, transpose your answers from the previous assessment into the key on the following page using the letters as a guide for the correct placement.

A   Represents where you will copy your HURTS

B   Represents where you will copy your EMPATHIC EXPECTATIONS

C   Represents where you will copy your ASSUMPTIONS

D   Represents where you will copy your REACTIONS

E   Represents where you will copy your TRIGGERS

_____
_____
_____
_____
_____
_____

Here are your key takeaways:

Believe it or not, I'm actually attracted to people who are...

A _____

yet I actually secretly HOPE they'll be

B _____

(That's probably unlikely at best.)

As a result, my painful assumption was that I had to be

C _____

otherwise love and approval might be taken away.

Understandably, I learned to react by

D _____

and that is exactly what prevents me from getting the love I deserve.

In the future, I need to remember that I am quite likely to be triggered by:

E _____

and this is a great sign that some healing may be required in this area in order for me to live my best life going forward.

Here's what your HEART Assessment may look like:
(based on my client, Melinda's example)

Believe it or not, I'm actually attracted to people who are…

<u>emotionally unavailable, lazy, unmotivated and accepted no responsibility</u>

yet I actually secretly HOPE they'll be

<u>dependable, hard-working and loyal</u>.

(That's probably unlikely at best.)

As a result, my painful assumption was that

<u>I didn't belong in my own family, I'd never be accepted and I'd be rejected and abandoned if I ever revealed who I was and how I felt</u>.

otherwise love and approval might be taken away.

Understandably, I learned to react by

<u>giving in, staying quiet for a very long time until I couldn't take it any more and then I would lash out angrily</u>

and that is exactly what prevents me from getting the love I deserve.

In the future, I need to remember that I am quite likely to be triggered by:

<u>feeling dismissed or ignored, ridiculed or yelled at unfairly</u>.

and this is a great sign that some healing may be required in this area
in order for me to live my best life going forward.

Introducing H.E.A.R.T. Flips™

The first thing I want to share with you is a little device I call H.E.A.R.T. Flips and I would define that as literally the exact opposite of all the distinctions you've already identified. We already sort of started doing that when we used your original Hurts or wounds to choose your Empathic Expectation or what you wanted instead. Now we're just going to continue that process on the other 4 aspects of the H.E.A.R.T. Assessment which we framed in the negative. While we will address that Empathic Expectation, there's really no need to flip it because it's already framed in the positive. So that means we're going to flip the following items in order to find an empowering truth. And don't worry if my directions seem confusing at first. I'm going to walk you through a number of examples in the book so it will quickly become obvious and pretty easy. Plus if you're using my *Companion Peace* workbook, you'll be able to simply fill in the blanks on the forms I created just for you and this exercise.

Hurts - You originally identified 3 wounds or disappointments from your childhood and we're going to flip that in order to find a compelling gift or blessing that came directly as a result of that hurt. Plus remember in each of these 4 areas; we want it to be a Class III scenario that makes the story serve you, serve others and serve the greater good.

Assumptions - You also identified 3 assumptions you made based on your beliefs about those wounds and what it meant about you as a child. Now with the clarity of time, wisdom and this all new awareness I've given you, we're going to dig back into these "stories" you told yourself and we're going to harvest a new and improved TRUTH that will serve you instead of debilitate you. The goal, here, is to help you consciously create what you want by putting you at CAUSE, rather than at EFFECT where you are powerless and at the mercy of whatever happens.

Reactions - You identified 3 ways your old disempowered reactions sabotaged you due to your lack of understanding based on what you knew at the time. Now that you have a new awareness and a lifetime of adult experience, you will now have an opportunity to CONSCIOUSLY CHOOSE how you will COMMIT to RESPONDING instead of unconsciously reacting. This is literally the strategic equivalent of deciding in advance what will work and what you want instead of just settling for what your old triggered responses and sabotage created.

Triggers - You identified three triggers that, in the past, have brought out the worst in you rather than your best. As I have shared and as you would expect, when you are emotionally triggered by some unresolved wound from your past, you don't respond from a grounded, centered and calm place. You respond from anger, rage, fear or resentment. These are hardly the building blocks of what I like to call a Legendary Love For Life or an effective partnership. (Coincidentally, that's also the name of my relationship coaching business.) I'm going to show you how to consciously choose your response in advance from an empowered state rather than an unconscious reaction from a disempowered state. That kind of flip is literally as profound as night and day.

Here's The Answer Key for your H.E.A.R.T. Flip:

- When we fill in the blanks, (1a), (2a) and (3a) are harvested from the 3 Hurts portion of the H.E.A.R.T. Assessment. The blank lines at (1b), (2b) and (3b) are the flips where you will create new empowering meanings.

- Line (4) is from the Empathic Expectation and it's already framed in the positive so there's no need to flip it. Just paste it.

- Lines (5a), (6a) and (7a) are harvested from the 3 Assumptions portion of the H.E.A.R.T. Assessment. The blank lines at (5b), (6b) and (7b) are the flips where you will redefine what else those assumptions could mean from an empowered and wiser place.

- Lines (8a), (9a), (10a) are harvested from the 3 Reactions portion of the H.E.A.R.T. Assessment. The blank lines at (8b), (9b), (10b) are the flips where you will now decide and commit to how you will Respond from an empowered place in the future instead of reacting from the old, wounded place.

- Lines (11a), (12a), (13a) are harvested from the 3 Triggers portion of the H.E.A.R.T. Assessment. The blank lines at (11b), (12b), (13b) are the flips where you will now decide and commit to how you will Respond from an empowered place in the future instead of reacting from the old, wounded place.

Now that we have the answer key out of the way, let's get started.

Although I was an innocent child at the time these beliefs were originally created, here's what I now know for sure in my H.E.A.R.T. and commit to practicing daily:

The truth is: any time I feel like someone is (1a) _____

that simply means that (1b) _____

_____

And any time I feel like someone is (2a) _____ I know for sure that

(2b) _____

_____

And when someone is (3a) _____, I just need to remember that

(3b) _____

_____

.

Despite all of this, I know beyond the shadow of a doubt that I will be healed when I know I was loved, am loved, and AM LOVABLE just as I am right now. I also know I have plenty of examples where people were (4) _____

_____ so I definitely know what that looks like and I deserve it!

Even though my assumption was that I (5a) _____, that is not true

because (5b) _____

_____.

And despite my assumption that (6a) _____, the truth is that

(6b) _____

_____

Lastly, whenever I think about my assumptions like (7a) _____

_____, I just need to remember that (7b) _____

_____

While I understand why the child in me used to (8a) _____,

I now know that the real answer lies in (8b) _____

_____.

Plus while it's reasonable that a child would feel forced to (9a) _____,

I now know that the real answer lies in (9b) _____

_____

.

And, of course, while a child might predictably (10a) _____,

I know that the real answer lies in (10b) _____

_____

Now whenever I get triggered by (11a) _____, I know that

(11b) _____

_____

In the future, when I get triggered by (12a) _____, I commit that I will

(12b) _____

_____

And whenever I feel triggered by (13a) _____, I can always

(13b) _____

_____

This is my solemn promise and commitment to myself & others. And so it is…

Signed: _____   Date: _____

Use this sample to create your own H.E.A.R.T. Flip:

Melinda's H.E.A.R.T. Flip:

Although I was an innocent child at the time these beliefs were originally created, here's what I now know for sure in my H.E.A.R.T. and commit to practicing daily:

The truth is, any time I feel like someone is (1a) <u>emotionally unavailable</u>, that simply means that (1b) <u>they're doing the best they can with what they have in the moment</u>.
And any time I feel like someone is (2a) <u>lazy and unmotivated</u>, I know for sure that (2b) <u>people's actions are a reflection of their beliefs and experience and that has nothing to do with me</u>.
And when someone is (3a) <u>accepting no responsibility</u>, I just need to remember that (3b) <u>what may bother me the most about that is that I've probably done something similar and I hate when I do it also. So that makes it a perfect mirror for me to examine my own behavior</u>.

Despite all of this, I know beyond shadow of a doubt that I will be healed when I know I was loved, am loved, and *am lovable* just as I am right now.
I also know I have plenty of examples where people were (4) <u>dependable, hard-working and loyal</u> so I definitely know what that looks like and I deserve it!

Even though my assumption was that I (5a) <u>didn't belong in my own family</u>, that is not true because (5b) <u>there have been many examples of where I've been embraced, loved and supported by family members</u>.
And despite my assumption that (6a) <u>I'd never be accepted</u>, the truth is that (6b) <u>feeling accepted by others is simply a reflection of how much I accept *myself*</u>!
Lastly, whenever I think about my assumptions like (7a) <u>my fear that I'd be rejected and abandoned</u>, I just need to remember that (7b) <u>while that is perfectly understandable, the problem with assumptions is that they make an ass out of you and me. (ass + u + me)</u>

While I understand why the child in me used to (8a) <u>give in and give up</u>, I now know that the real answer lies in (8b) <u>getting clear on my outcome and asking myself better quality questions about what's really important to me</u>.
Plus while it's reasonable that a child would feel forced to (9a) <u>stay quiet</u>, I now know that the real answer lies in (9b) <u>speaking my truth from an empowered place and asking for what I want</u>.
And, of course, while a child might predictably (10a) <u>lash out angrily</u>, I know that the real answer lies in (10b) <u>taking back the power I now own as an adult who makes good decisions</u>.

Now whenever I get triggered by (11a) <u>feeling dismissed or ignored</u>, I know that (11b) <u>is a great reminder to me about raising my standards and speaking my truth</u>.
In the future, when I get triggered by (12a) <u>feeling ridiculed</u>, I commit that I will (12b) <u>speak up and demand better or use my power to walk away for good if necessary</u>.
And whenever I feel triggered by (13a) <u>being yelled at unfairly</u>, I can always (13b) <u>take back my power by enforcing a boundary and walking away</u>.

This is my solemn promise and commitment to myself and others. And so it is.

Chapter 9:

The ABC's of Healing

In my ABC's of Change, the A stands for **Aspirations**.

Since I just finished writing about the pleasure of achievement or fulfillment, now seems like a good time to consider the idea of your Aspirations. This is where we begin to identify what, specifically, would bring you great pleasure and make you feel proud when it comes to finding love and passion in your life. What kind of relationship do you long to have when you meet your love? How do you want to feel in your relationship? What kinds of things will you celebrate together? Where would you love to go with your partner? What ideas excite you and kind of make your heart race when you think about achieving them together? What's in your heart to achieve before your time on earth is complete? What do you fantasize about sharing with your partner in your mind's eye? Who do you admire or wish you could emulate in terms of their relationship? What legacy of love would you aspire to create? These are just a few of the questions that will help you hone in on what would keep you motivated on that path toward your dreams.

It's like a chance to leave the world better than you found it. Perhaps you've heard the old saying that the two best days in your life are the day you're born and the day you figure out why. In other words, it's a recognition of the power of how your own self-actualization leads you to finding your calling in life. It's almost like the challenging experience itself was somehow pre-ordained by fate in order to help you discover your purpose or destiny. destiny? So, if this is a powerful predictor, what would you say was your "hero's journey" and what did it come to teach you?

What Aspirations Inspire You & Make You Excited?

A "Hero's Journey" generally features a story of a humble protagonist who faces some sort of monumental obstacle that challenges him or her to the core and fundamentally transforms the main character into a hero. Then, once a hero rises to this challenge and conquers it, the compulsion to use that experience and pay it forward is powerful. It's like a chance to leave the world better than you found it. What would you say was your "hero's journey" & what did it come to teach you?

What Are Your Aspirations of Love?

We're all here for a reason. What's your reason? What is the mission you're here to achieve when it comes to love?

If you could only do one thing with your time on earth, what will you leave behind as your legacy of love?

Ask yourself: "How can I create even more love right now?" "How can I do/be/have _____?" Trust the process and know that the answer will come in due time when you ask in the exact way I just showed you

The second phase of the ABC's of Healing stands for

Benefits

In this phase of the ABC's, we want to continue to stack the benefits in a way that feels good to you and motivates you to do what it takes to stay on track. Again, whatever we link pleasure to has the power to keep us focused in the direction of the dreams we want to create. When you're clear on the benefit of what you want and why, that can be the difference between hitting a snooze button on your alarm or sitting in front of a TV for endless hours instead of taking some kind of clear and productive action in the direction of your dreams. Stacking the benefits will get you to commit to doing an online dating profile instead of just talking about it. It'll get you out of your house and enjoying life instead of sitting around waiting for something great to happen when you haven't done anything to MAKE things happen. It'll get you to the gym or help you make good, nourishing food choices because you're clear on the importance of your own health. In the book, I made the assumption that since you picked up my book, perhaps having an inspiring and fulfilling love was something you wanted and I created a sample list of 50 Benefits to having a love like that. You're welcome to use that and adopt it as-is, OR you can use it as a starting point and create your own OR you can make up your own list for this or any other purpose you wish. It's all about the power of the Compelling Future:

- What excites you and serves as your powerful why?
- What do you find incredibly fulfilling?
- What would you love to create as your legacy?
- What would make you proud to look back on years from now?
- What would you love other people to say about you?

Take some time to stack the benefits of an incredible life lived with purpose on the following pages. Feel free to add more paper and journal if you wish. This your life. There are no limits.

The Benefits of Love

1. Every single feature in your "human highlight reel" will be an act of love.
2. Love is the ultimate guidepost for navigating a life well-lived.
3. Love magnifies the experience of life and enhances it.
4. Love divides the sorrow or pain so you don't suffer alone.
5. A loving partner can provide support through challenging times.
6. Experiencing love can make you emotionally healthier.
7. Experiencing love can make you physically healthier.
8. Those who share love tend to live longer, happier lives.
9. A loving relationship can provide emotional intimacy.
10. A loving relationship can provide physical intimacy.
11. A loving relationship can lead to creating a family.
12. Giving love to others is a beautiful game-changer for you.
13. Giving love to others is a beautiful game-changer for them.
14. Demonstrating loving behaviors is a positive influence on your own family.
15. Demonstrating loving behaviors is a positive influence on the world.
16. Having love in your life creates magic moments.
17. Love is the centerpiece for every social celebration.
18. Love is the currency that is exchanged between family and friends.
19. Love creates a community where you can feel at home.
20. Love creates a feeling of safety.
21. Love leads to acceptance and understanding.
22. Love can build a bridge to any destination.
23. Love is your connection to the presence of spirit.
24. When you're connected to spirit, you're connected to love.
25. When you have love, you're never alone.
26. Love and gratitude go together hand-in-hand.
27. Love and happiness increase your odds of finding meaningful work.
28. When you know love, you can know peace. (No love, no peace.)
29. Love is the energy that can attract every good thing to you.
30. Love and passion are closely aligned, so one can lead to the other.
31. The power of love can lead you to your mission.
32. Being in a relationship can multiply your income.
33. Being in a relationship can greatly cut your expenses.
34. Love and money can raise your standard of living.
35. Having love in your life makes you far more resilient.
36. Love literally makes your life about something bigger than just you.
37. Love is a building block for a life of joy.
38. Love is the root of patience and compassion.
39. Love can also give you the leverage to set and enforce healthy boundaries.
40. Acting in love will always keep you on track even when it's hard.
41. Love releases endorphins, dopamine and other pleasure chemicals in your brain.
42. Having love in your heart keeps you youthful and vibrant at any age.
43. Love is the secret ingredient in "regret repellent."
44. A loving smile enhances anyone's looks.
45. When you learn how to love unconditionally, you have mastered life.
46. Acts of love are the basis for all morality.
47. Love is, and always has been, your birthright and your natural state.
48. When you're not sure what to do, ask "what would love do now?" Then do it.
49. Having love in your life makes every single day better. No exceptions.
50. Living with love in your heart is the ultimate success!

What Are The Benefits Of You Living Your Very Best Life?

What Are The Benefits Of You Living Your Very Best Life?

1. What would you add to this list if it was yours? _____

_____

_____

_____

2. What benefits of love do you see? _____

_____

_____

_____

3. What benefits do you offer a partner? _____

_____

_____

_____

4. Why are you committed to having a love of your own? _____

_____

_____

_____

5. What are you willing to do to have love? _____

_____

_____

_____

The third phase of the ABC's of Healing stands for

Costs

The final feature in The ABC's of Healing is designed to get you clear on the Costs of NOT doing what needs to be done in order to have what you want. While this is similar to what we did in Chapter 8 when we got clear on the leverage for why we must do this work now, that chapter was more macro in its "big picture" approach to why we should do the work. For the Cost portion of the ABC's, that's more of a micro version of the smaller, more specific goal here. Again, when we created the list of Benefits, that was predicated on WHY you might want to learn to attract the love of your life and how it might make your life presumably better. So if you want a simple tip here for clarity, the COST of not doing this work will essentially be **THE EXACT OPPOSITE** of the benefits. In other words, if you don't dig in and do the work, it will potentially cost you every single thing you may have been excited about wanting.

In the book, I made the assumption that since you picked up my book, perhaps having an inspiring and fulfilling was something you wanted and I created a sample list of 50 Benefits to having a love like that. You're welcome to use that and adopt it as-is, OR you can use it as a starting point and create your own OR you can make up your own list for this or any other purpose you wish.

Just as a reminder, in the book, I simply copied the list of 50 benefits and reversed them in order to illustrate what you'll potentially miss out on your life if you don't step up and do this now. You can feel free to do the same with your list.

Again, the benefit is that motivation that comes with a push away from pain – and a pull toward pleasure – tends to be very effective.

1) What's going to happen if you don't address this now?

_____
_____
_____

2) What's it going to cost you?

_____
_____
_____

3) What will you never get to experience?

_____
_____
_____

4) Where will you never get to go or enjoy?

_____
_____
_____

5) Who won't be in your life any more?

_____
_____
_____

6) Who will never show up because of this?

_____
_____
_____

7) Who might get disgusted or frustrated and just give up on you?

_____
_____

8) What will that do to your health?

___

___

___

9) How miserable will you be if this doesn't change?

___

___

___

10) What do you think this problem is doing to your finances?

___

___

___

11) How might this affect your faith or spirituality?

___

___

___

12) What's going to happen to you if you can't find faith or believe in something?

___

___

___

13) Who might leave your family if you don't solve this?

_____
_____
_____

14) Who's going to start avoiding you…or just stop coming around?

_____
_____
_____

15) How is this affecting your career?

_____
_____
_____

16) What job are you going to be stuck in because of this?

_____
_____
_____

17) What job or opportunity are you never going to get?

_____
_____
_____

18) What will your colleagues think about you?

_____
_____
_____

19) What about your boss?

_____
_____
_____

20) What's going to happen if you keep settling?

_____
_____
_____

21) What's life going to look like if you never speak up or tell the truth?

_____
_____
_____

22) If we don't change this NOW, how much worse will it be a year from now?

_____
_____
_____

23) How about two years from now if nothing changes?

_____
_____
_____

24) What if it goes five more years without a change?

_____
_____

25) Where will your health be then?

26) Who will have just had it by then and walk away?

27) How about your finances after five more years of this?

28) What kind of shape do you think you'll be in a decade from now?

29) Imagine. Another ten years of this. Are you okay with that?

30) How do you think you're going to age with this kind of stress?

31) Imagine 10 more years of this strain on your health. Will anyone be there to take care of you?

32) Imagine how tired and worn out you'll be after 10 more years of this crap…

33) How about fifteen more years of this?

34) What about 20 YEARS from now…what chance will be gone forever by then?

35) Now stack on another five years of regret…25 years of wasted chances.

36) How are you going to live with the fact that you didn't even try?

37) What's going to happen when your window of opportunity closes for good?

38) How will it feel to know that opportunity knocked and you didn't answer?

39) What are you doing to when it's too late to live your dream?

40) How are you going to explain to people why you never took a shot?

41) How will you live with the guilt of your poor decisions?

42) What kind of shame are you going to feel if you don't take action now?

_____
_____
_____

43) What are you going to regret 30 years from now if you don't just do it?

_____
_____
_____

44) Who will you never get to meet because of your fear?

_____
_____
_____

45) What is your lack of faith going to cost you that you'll never experience?

_____
_____
_____

46) What will your life be like 40 years from now? 50? 80?

_____
_____
_____

47) How much longer are you going to play small and settle for mediocrity?

_____
_____
_____

48) What regrets are you going to take to your grave?

_____
_____
_____

49) What are people going to say about you when you're gone?

_____
_____
_____

50) What would it feel like to meet the person you could have been?

_____
_____
_____

Sorry about that…

Okay, I apologize if that stirred up some pain. I promise you, though – there is a reason why I asked you do that. First, I want you to know that you are not brittle or weak. If you're reading this, you made it through the tough part and you're still here. So acknowledge yourself and your own innate toughness. Well done! Secondly, I want you to be really clear on why these old fears, stories and insecurities MUST change now. You deserve to be free and you can't – or won't – get there if you're not 100% committed to taking action and doing what is necessary to get the result. The choice is and has always been yours.

What Are The Costs Of You NOT Stepping Up Right Now & Why Is This A Must?

Chapter 10:

Same Old Story –

Brand New Happy Ending

The 12 Traumatic M.I.S.B.E.H.A.V.I.O.R.S.™

If you know my work, you know that I tend to use acronyms to unpack a large amount of related information. I find it just helps me to remember it as I'm teaching it plus it helps the people who are learning it to recall it also. That's why I've organized a list I call The 12 Traumatic M.I.S.B.E.H.A.V.I.O.R.S.™ that are directly and most often responsible for these wounds that often linger deep in the receiver's subconscious well into adulthood. You can pretty much think of these (mis)behaviors as "the dirty dozen;" outrageous acts of abuse inflicted on innocent and practically defenseless children. Perhaps worst of all, these acts aren't usually perpetrated by shadowy strangers with ill intent. The truth is, they're usually inflicted by trusted adults including the parents, caretakers, family members or other adult authority figures who are well known to the child who is victimized. To be clear, in this case, the "child" we're talking about is probably you. Some of you may not like these behaviors described as "trauma-inducing" because it may make it sound worse than you want it to sound. While I never want to make anything worse than it is, only better, I also want to be clear that you are not over-reacting in any way if some of these misbehaviors have left you with sensitivities, insecurities, fear or even harm many years later. In fact, it's these ACTIONS that have directly lead to the less-than-helpful thoughts, beliefs and behaviors that have the power to haunt you years and decades later. I'd much rather acknowledge them as legitimate than pretend they didn't exist because that LITERALLY is the path to taking back your power: you feel what you feel and do it anyway because no one else gets to define you. That's your job and yours alone.

The 12 Traumatic M.I.S.B.E.H.A.V.I.O.R.S.

Manipulation

Injustice

Shame

Betrayal

Exploitation

Humiliation

Abandonment

Violence

Isolation

Objectification

Rejection

Sexual assault

Now that you have a new understanding of the Twelve Traumatic MISBEHAVIORS, it will help to actually take this content and turn it into powerful, compelling exercises that will strengthen you. Here's a simple format that can help you transform from an awareness to a commitment – and that's where all the power is to set you free and move you forward into the kind of life and love you deserve. Simply use this format and as you begin to fill in the blanks, you will also begin to find the resolve to find freedom.

(Turn the page for a sample of how to fill in the form).

If I forever fault _____ for _____,

I would miss out on the following gifts and benefits:

_____

_____

_____

Instead of simply holding a grudge that punishes me, I CHOOSE to believe this:

_____

_____

_____

And I COMMIT to do this:

_____

_____

_____

This is the gift I give to myself because I deserve it.

It is written. It is resolved. It is done. (Date) _____

Signed: _____

Sample Commitment:

If I forever fault <u>my dad</u> for <u>manipulating me to feel like I was a bad child</u>,

I would miss out on the following gifts and benefits:
I never would have developed the strength to know for sure that I wasn't bad,
I never would have learned to think for myself instead of believing everything I heard, I wouldn't have learned to believe in MYSELF and I might have become a quitter, I never would have become such a good and caring parent
I never would have discovered how good it feels to stand up for what's right!

Instead of simply holding a grudge, I CHOOSE to believe

My dad did the best he could with what he knew at the time.
If he had known better – or was raised better – he would have done better.
Despite it all, I know that he loved me the best way he knew

And I COMMIT to do this:

I will continue to BE the change I wish to see in the world by being understanding, accepting people where they are, loving them without agenda and I will do my best to model the love and forgiveness I WANT to feel!

This is the gift I give to myself because I deserve it.
It is written. It is resolved. It is done. (Date) _____

Signed: _____

Chapter 11:

Knowing & Showing Your Value – The 8 F's of Personal Transformation

These eight F words (no, not that one!) I'm about to share represent the eight major sectors or components of a life well-lived. In each of these individual sectors, we both expend energy and receive energy. When an individual area consumes more energy than it provides on a regular basis, it will operate at a deficit and over time, it will deplete you. However, if an area creates more energy than it consumes, you operate at a surplus and the net effect is that you will feel empowered.

Friends

Family

Fun

Focus

Fitness

Fulfillment

Finance

Faith

On a scale of 1-10, how am I doing in the area of _____?

FRIENDS SCORE: _____ **out of 10**

Notes on final score:

Here's where I'm doing great in the area of friends:

_____

_____

_____

Here's what I should consider changing:

_____

_____

_____

Random notes/thoughts:

_____

_____

_____

FAMILY SCORE: _____ **out of 10**

Notes on final score:

Here's where I'm doing great in the area of family:

_____

Here's what I should consider changing:

Random notes/thoughts:

FUN SCORE: _____ **out of 10**

Notes on final score:

Here's where I'm doing great in the area of fun:

Here's what I should consider changing:

Random notes/thoughts:

FOCUS SCORE: _____ out of 10

Notes on final score:

Here's where I'm doing great in the area of focus:

Here's what I should consider changing:

Random notes/thoughts:

FITNESS SCORE: _____ **out of 10**

Notes on final score:

Here's where I'm doing great in the area of fitness:

_____

_____

_____

Here's what I should consider changing:

_____

_____

_____

Random notes/thoughts:

_____

_____

_____

FULFILLMENT SCORE: _____ **out of 10**

Notes on final score:

Here's where I'm doing great in the area of fulfillment:

_____

_____

_____

Here's what I should consider changing:

_____

_____

_____

Random notes/thoughts:

_____

_____

_____

FINANCE SCORE: _____ **out of 10**

Notes on final score:

Here's where I'm doing great in the area of finance:

_____

_____

_____

Here's what I should consider changing:

_____

_____

_____

Random notes/thoughts:

___

FAITH SCORE: _____ **out of 10**

Notes on final score:

Here's where I'm doing great in the area of faith:

___

Here's what I should consider changing:

___

Random notes/thoughts:

___

The Key

8-30	We have some work to do so let's get started!
31-40	I'm really glad you're doing this exercise - great things ahead!
41-50	You're in a great position to make some real shifts!
51-60	Good job and we have some room to grow!
61-70	Tremendous job on a high-quality life!
71-80	This is incredible! Congratulations on a life well-lived!

_____   Total number of points

Now that you have your total, you can get an all-new understanding of where you are in this moment. Remember, whether you love your score or you think it's low, it is nothing more than a snapshot of a moment in time. The good news is that in the next chapter, I'm going to walk you through some game-changing exercises that can make a tremendous difference in both your life and in the life of others in your circle.

Your Total Score In The 8 F's: _____

Chapter 12:

Growing Your Greatness – The 8 F's of Personal Transformation

Once you identify your lowest scoring area out of the 8 F's, which is the low hanging fruit, that's obviously where the biggest turnarounds are possible. That's when you ask yourself,

"What are maybe 3 things you can commit to right now that would help improve that area for you?"

Once you do that, you go through the process again. If you can take a 5 out of 10, for instance, and come up with some new targeted action that addresses your biggest concerns, oftentimes you can get that 5 out of 10 up to an 8 out of 10, that can add up to a huge change.

Then if you repeat that process for each of the 8 areas, you can multiply your growth exponentially.

Friends　　　　　　　　　Areas for improvement

　　　　　　　　　　　　　　1) _____

Original score ____ /10　　2) _____

Revised score ____ /10　　3) _____

Family　　　　　　　　　Areas for improvement

　　　　　　　　　　　　　　1) _____

Original score ____ /10　　2) _____

Revised score ____ /10　　3) _____

Fun　　　　　　　　　　Areas for improvement

　　　　　　　　　　　　　　1) _____

Original score ____ /10　　2) _____

Revised score ____ /10　　3) _____

Focus　　　　　　　　　Areas for improvement

　　　　　　　　　　　　　　1) _____

Original score ____ /10　　2) _____

Revised score ____ /10　　3) _____

Fitness   Areas for improvement

                                     1) _____

Original score _____ / 10   2) _____

Revised score _____ / 10   3) _____

Fulfillment   Areas for improvement

                                     1) _____

Original score _____ / 10   2) _____

Revised score _____ / 10   3) _____

Finance   Areas for improvement

                                     1) _____

Original score _____ / 10   2) _____

Revised score _____ / 10   3) _____

Faith   Areas for improvement

                                     1) _____

Original score _____ / 10   2) _____

Revised score _____ / 10   3) _____

Friends: Revised score _____/10 = _____ Total increase

Family: Revised score _____/10 = _____ Total increase

Fun: Revised score _____/10 = _____ Total increase

Focus: Revised score _____/10 = _____ Total increase

Fitness: Revised score _____/10 = _____ Total increase

Fulfillment: Revised score _____/10 = _____ Total increase

Finance: Revised score _____/10 = _____ Total increase

Faith: Revised score _____/10 = _____ Total increase

New, Improved. Total Score for THE 8 F's of Personal Transformation

What Are Your Top Takeaways From This Book?

_____

_____

_____

_____

_____

_____

_____

_____

_____

_____

_____

_____

What Are Your Top Takeaways From This Book?

What Will Your Life Be Like When You've Done This Work?

What Are You Committed To Making Happen Now?

What Are The Costs Of You NOT Stepping Up Right Now?

Chapter 13:

 The Past May Predict Your Future but It's not Predetermined

Your Chapter Notes:

_____
_____
_____
_____
_____
_____
_____
_____
_____

About the Author:
Dave Elliott

When it comes to making sense of the often mystifying topic of relationships, Dave Elliott is an international relationship coach who breaks down complex concepts into easily understandable principles and practices.
Whether he's working one-on-one with a client, being interviewed by the media, writing an article that goes viral on the Internet or creating another relationship book or product, his advice is right on target because he tells it like it is and breaks it down in simple terms.

In his latest book, *Same Sh*t. Different Date.*, Dave uses that gift and ability to simplify the complex and bring the invisible to light in order to promote massive, life-changing healing for all who seek it. This book distills more than a decade of experience and education and multiple tens of thousands of hours spent working directly with, or on behalf of, thousands of clients and individuals into a methodology that will help them heal the lingering wounds that get in the way of them creating the life and love they deserve. This book is a culmination of what is now his life's work and a defining moment in a career dedicated to creating more love, peace and understanding in the world. It is not an overstatement to say this book is a profoundly powerful game-changer and a proud representation of Dave's legacy and mission.

Dave is known for getting results with a variety of techniques that enable rapid transformational change. With his experience and training, he helps teach others how to effectively understand, predict and even influence human behavior. Dave's main focus is helping people navigate the uncertainties of their most intimate relationships. His specialty is helping women learn to understand men and work with them much more effectively in order to bring out the very best in them rather than suffering through the worst from them. Plus as a Neurostrategist, he provides people with the awareness and specific strategies for success that they need in order to create success.

After his own marriage ended in a painful and disappointing divorce, Dave used that experience to drive him to discover just what it takes to create A Legendary Love for Life, which is, coincidentally, the name of his coaching business. After researching and learning about everything he could find in the field of human relationships, he took the very best information he found and perfected it to make it easier to learn, more memorable and even more effective.

The good news is that on his journey, he met and married a woman who shared his commitment to mastering the area of relationships. Today, he and his wife, Katrina, share a mission to travel the world to touch, move and inspire others in healing their own wounds and forming more conscious, loving and evolved relationships. Together, they look forward to perhaps meeting you at an upcoming seminar or presentation.

In addition to sharing his expertise on TV, on radio, live on stage and as a highly sought-after expert blogger on popular relationship Web sites, Dave has also created and markets his own personal line of products.

His first book, *The Catch Your Match Formula*™, was inspired by the fact that Dave saw too many good people struggle in their dating lives because they were having trouble standing out from the crowd and connecting deeply with other singles. As a result, he set out to write a book that would give people a smart, real-world and no-nonsense approach to building rapport both online and in person. His background in coaching and as an award-winning advertising copywriter was filled with a whole toolbox of professional-quality tools that could be taught easily and effectively in order to make a huge difference quickly and end their struggle. Today, years later, there are many real-world couples who met, got engaged and even married after using the strategies Dave shared in that book. He also has dozens of clients who have used his help to meet their fiancé's and husbands and have become proud members of what is affectionately known as his Very Satisfied Client Club.™

His rapid relationship turnaround CD, known as *The H.U.G. & K.I.S.S. Hierarchy*, will help you elicit and unlock your partner's – or your own – exact love and attraction strategy. This technique is incredibly powerful and transformational because it gives you the exact combination that will open your partner's heart any and every time so they feel loved in exactly the way they NEED to be loved.

In addition, he's also the Creator of The ManMagnetics Formula™ – a free Web site that teaches women the nine secrets to bring out the very best in men so they can avoid settling for the worst. You can learn all about it and watch hours of free video instruction at www.manmagnetics.com.

Currently, Dave and his wife, Katrina, are back in Dave's hometown of Baltimore, Maryland in the United States but they will also be returning to their other home in Australia. When they're not traveling, teaching or coaching, they're usually renovating a house, investing in properties or spending time with their friends and family, including their amazing grandson, nephew and niece whom they adore.

Made in the USA
Las Vegas, NV
14 October 2021